POEMS
BY BRANDON
FLESHER

POEMS
BY BRANDON
FLESHER

BRANDON FLESHER

authorHOUSE®

AuthorHouse™
1663 Liberty Drive
Bloomington, IN 47403
www.authorhouse.com
Phone: 1-800-839-8640

Cover photo taken by Brandon Flesher

Published by AuthorHouse   04/03/2012

ISBN: 978-1-4685-5769-5 (sc)
ISBN: 978-1-4685-5768-8 (hc)
ISBN: 978-1-4685-5767-1 (e)

Library of Congress Control Number: 2012903709

Any people depicted in stock imagery provided by Thinkstock are models, and such images are being used for illustrative purposes only.
Certain stock imagery © Thinkstock.

This book is printed on acid-free paper.

I would like to dedicate this book to all the friends in my life and my family. You have all left an imprint on me and I would like to thank you for the joys as well as the headaches given no matter how small they seemed or large, I am truly lucky to have you and have known you. And to Sean Singleton, a life cut to short. Lastly I would like to dedicate this book to all those who have travelled to the dark places within themselves and who fear they are alone, please keep treading the waters because you never know what tomorrow brings.

ONE

Enclosed within these polished walls
The sight of freedom so near
Jumping and clawing
Resisting and yelling
I try to free myself in vain
Enclosed within my mind
These walls so shear
Looking for an escape
And when I cast away this weight
Only to realize
That we are tethered as one
In hopeless indifference I struggle
Only to tire the more quickly
In exhaustion I yield
Falling deeper within
In realization
As the dawning of a new day come slowly
That which confined me
Was born from that which emancipated me

FIVE

As a sculpture cast in ice
So to was your love
Your skin glowing in the noonday sun
But cold to the touch
Your shape as flowing as that of water
But as unforgiving as ice
As a thing of beauty
One is awed by your appearance
Only to see right through
Thinking that you are strong
Only to crack and break
As ice is want to do
And in the warmth of my love
You began to melt
Only to melt away from me

ELEVEN

Without direction
As a ship set sail
And once a course plotted
Abandoned
Fore the sight of land was lost
And the heavens were clouded
Without the use of markers
The heart lost
Direction unknown
Thought mutinied
And in silence
The heavens cleared
Without thought
Without direction
Alone at sea
Abandoned

SEVENTEEN

Trying to capture the spirit of the moment
Within the vagueness of presentation
For how can one convey the subtleties of thought
In the concreteness of fruition
For in the flirtation
The meaning is lost

EIGHTEEN

Withering with time
The flower fades
Its colors blend
Its once soft pedals
Crumble and fall
Upright once
It now bends
To a will not its own
Witnessed
In passing
Remembered
Withered
In time
Forgotten

TWENTY SEVEN

In Memory of Sean David Singleton

1974-1999

The spark in your eyes
Was beauty
A flicker as warm as the sun
For something we could not comprehend
For a brief moment you had touched heaven
Only to fall
As man is befallen to do
The spark now gone
Irretrievable in dejection
For something we could not comprehend
A life cut short
For a love unfounded
Hope falling to deaf ears
For we did not comprehend
The strength of your love
And the depth of your passion

THIRTY SIX

A wall of silent trepidation sensed
But never touched
Unfathomable fear
Drawn from the greatest hope
The simplest fear
Which cometh from within
As brittle as virtue
As unfulfillable as vice
So to is your love
My heart in vice
Waiting for the throw of the dice

FORTY ONE

When love is forsaken
And all is cold
What fills the void is emptiness
Longing for what is bold
Grasping for what is cold
A sullen joyousness
A bitter playfulness
One learns to revel in pointlessness
As easily as one learns happiness

FORTY THREE

In longing
We clutch for what we have destroyed
Apathetic
As a child looking for security
From the familiar
In an unfamiliar world
And in comfort
We recover
But do we grow
Or does the shelter we seek
Only delay
In shadow clothed

FIFTY EIGHT

With the appearance of clarity
And the appearance of stability
One does not see the imperfections
Inherent in a bridge of ice
One wholeheartedly takes the first step
With silent trepidation
And after it falls
With vigor restored
One traverses the symbol with out heed
And with the crack of doubt
Shattering
The imperfections become clear
And in disbelief one shouts
"I was deceived!"
And the realization is realized
That one was awed by the spectacle
And deceived by the moment

SIXTY

A man awakens
To find himself in heaven
"How am I here?"
"Because we felt pity for your soul."
"Why?"
"Because you could not help your weakness."
"For what you call weakness I call strength."
"For I died for what I held as dear."
"Even in the face of judgment."
For then there was a crack of thunder
And the clouds were torn asunder
And an angel fallen

SEVENTY NINE

Is life a game of chance
If in fate we meet
For in chance do we seize our fate
Or in fate do we seize the chance

EIGHTY ONE

Man aspires in tragedy
But relishes in vanity
Revels in proclamation
Forgetting virtuosity
In indignation
Hiding in justification
Relentlessly pursuing
What was known all along
Indulging weakness
In acts of pettiness
With haughty compassion

EIGHTY FIVE

In a realm of glittering facades
Forever turning
And shimmering
Carousing thought
Numbing instinct
Is where we dance this silly dance
And when one tires
And seeks refuge
One begins to see
Only to become transfixed
Transfixed by the realm of glittering facades
To dance anew

NINETY FIVE

True love is work
For even a precious stone
Is cut and polished
In value

ONE HUNDRED EIGHT

In loneliness sought
Loneliness brought
A weighty burden
A mantle betrothed
In lonely musing
With such bemusing
In loneliness sought
Loneliness brought
A tender tear
Held to dear
From hidden fear

ONE HUNDRED TWENTY

The sorrow you sung
Fell to most unworthy ears
And hung from most untrustworthy tears
For heaven's bell
Thy soul had rung
To heaven's hell
Thy soul was flung
For your love was as boundless as the sea
And blind as night
Your love no fault could see
And in such way
Your love was entrust to she
Though heaven bent
Your love to she
Was cast aside
For the sorrow you sung
Fell to most unworthy ears
And the fears you quelled
Caused uncontrollable tears

ONE HUNDRED TWENTY ONE

With hope your love could cause compel
In deepest labyrinth of heart to dwell
But in haste
A love did waste
For in haste
One could not the deception taste
Hidden within love's sweet taste

ONE HUNDRED THIRTY

For love abide in me
Your gentle sleep
Till death in me
Confides to me
It's gentle sleep
For from sleep deprived
My mind does ride
To glistening keep
Upon a mountain hide
To lowly place
To dark to reside
But love does cause this great divide
And scorch my heart
Unable to chide
Though piteous be
My heart to me
No pity is asked of you
From me
I know
In love
It was not to be
But love abide in me your gentle sleep
Till death in me
It's promise keep

ONE HUNDRED THIRTY SEVEN

Heaven
Cast your light from me
For in your light
I now can see what was once dark
And held no relevancy
Your light
Unknowing heaven
Shines upon it's relevancy
So I beseech
Upon bended knee
Cast your shadow upon me
And in this shadow
I may reckon me

ONE HUNDRED FORTY THREE

My mind in fear does threaten me
For from itself it does me kneed
This perceived self-doubt, so keen in it's prowess,
And possessed of crushing clout
Springs forth from spring traversed, unbecoming of time
Begetting itself with affluent indignation,
In forsaken a clime
And all my fears taken in with the salty bitterness of brine
Swim within this spring
Sprung forth from time
And woe be gone, my angry heart, trodden upon in detestable mind
And hope in the hope, that the
Fountainhead will collapse in time

ONE HUNDRED FORTY FOUR

Is this the Devil's hand I perceive,
Upon my heart, in this cold breast
Alive to me.
Or is this an illusion made, so I can reconcile my sullen way
For if the Devil it be, no blame shall lay upon me
For the Devil's hand will cloak my heart with Devil's brand,
And relinquish me from the blame of this barren and arid land
My heart is to me.
But lo, woe will belong to me if the Devil's hand it not be.
For then this hand constricting be will belong to me,
And I will be the one to which this hand so desolate and bereft has sprung.
Then this woe, which oppresses so mercilessly as the desert noon sun,
Belongs to me and solely from within me.
For no cause to blame other than me.
And so I run and beseech of thee
For a cause not of me, oh please.
But if this cause spring from me
Then I be dwelling in the land of hypocrisy
So I hope the hope the cause the Devil it be
And not born within me, even if unknowingly
But nay, this hand which destroys me must not be mine.
For then the Devil's soul, his and mine be twine.
And the cause for my dissent lands within me, and I, so simple be,
Am the only cause for this trouble to me.

ONE HUNDRED FORTY FIVE

To descend into hollow glee and revelry, and sing these praise uproariously.
Then to scurry within and make a castle to reside,
And goto in times of needed hide.
For when the weight unto you is to unbearable for you
To burden staunchly.
You travel to within to escape your self brought plight.
For all without is cause for this plights delight.
And there in your castle do you hide.
This place so serene,
All the cause is washed of you and no blame can hold unto you.
To again descend into hollow glee and revelry,
And sing these praises uproariously.
Until love's gentle sting be felt.
And this game before you melts.
So within you run.
For the game, no longer,
Is fun.

ONE HUNDRED FORTY SIX

This thing within my heart
Sagging breath, morose part
From where it came
This morose part
From days of old
Before the cold
And yet it stays
For a love not yet met
This morose part
Waiting for the love
To melt this heart

ONE HUNDRED FORTY NINE

The divine comedy lies within life
For life springs from the divine
And a comedy through tragedy defined
For the sun and moon do dance their dance
Through ages
And within man's heart do light
The fires of sages
But the sun and moon do dance
Their dances without thought of progression
And man will boast his firm grasp of conception
Even though he realizes not his deception
For night is day and day is night
Each begetting the other in succession
And becoming either
Understood from perception
And within this distinction
Lies no cause for affection
For upon this road well travelled
Lies many a twist and turn well trodden
But all to none
For soon we are forgotten
And the sun and moon will dance
Their dance through ages
And care not of our stages
Even though their light does play
Upon our faces

FALLEN (ONE HUNDRED FIFTY ONE)

Upon a sunken angel love does frown
For upon their head love once did crown
For the love once held did shine as bright
Through soul thought meld
From sky so high
To lowly field
And from this love the angel did wield their purpose.
And sprung from purpose the angel did soar
Above the roar of earthly plight
And observe this world thru heavenly sight
But what through heaven's love shines brilliantly bright.
Thru heaven's scorn lays wasted in spite.
For thru this love heaven did impale with confessional wail
Yet to no avail
This heaven sent wail.
The heart already be stung
And to hell is flung
For upon the sunken angel love does frown
For upon their head love once did crown.

ONE HUNDRED FIFTY NINE

In lust one feels the just
For lust does cause the heart to combust
And from these flames
Which burn so bright
Cloaking all with shimmering light
The heart does swell with feelings delight
For lust does seek to console the hearts appeal
But lust does lie
To itself conceal
And lust lays waste to that which one holds
Silently dear
For lust
As haste, makes waste through it's zeal
The heart above mind in feelings real
The fire dies
No longer real

ONE HUNDRED SIXTY SEVEN

Within these simple lines
Lies a feeble attempt to grasp
What lies in time
For with little wit
In something writ
Only to try to unravel life's rhyme
And in due time
A lowly clime
Servant to the mind
Free from itself
Trapped within a game making lame
For within these simple lines
In do time
My soul be held
Trapped within searching line

A TALK (ONE HUNDRED SEVENTY SIX)

I saw a man
Who walked with me
He said in life there is happiness
But then I saw his face
Then why do look unhappy I said
Love, he stated
Then he laughed
Then he smiled
Why do you smile then
Love, he stated

ONE HUNDRED EIGHTY

I am sorry
Sorry for what
For being true to you
Sorry would be living for another
And not for you
Sorry is a word when there is nothing left
How shallow this word
Which is so inept
So forget this word and feelings of regret
For being true to self releases all from debt
And take wing and alight
For to your heart you do right
And think not of my sorry plight
So forget these words which inadequate be
And live high and forget me
And think not of my plight
Self brought on me
For the love I tried to make be

ONE HUNDRED NINETY

Exiled from heaven
And sent to hell
In hope
Holds no compare
For it holds the despair
In indulgence asked
No thought to dare
A loved one rejected
Cast away
Through petulance astray
For spite does hold an unredeemable scepter
Become such a ponderous specter
For even smoke
Which from the fire does burn
Released from yoke
To heaven shall turn

ONE HUNDRED NINETY EIGHT

Within the cave of knowing
I took fright
For the blight within my sight
Seemed to radiate light
As black as night
What was beholden to me
Was no longer golden to me
But black as coal
And hard as stone
For from within
A blackened moan
The obsidian stone
Mirrored to me
The fears in me
For this fright
As black as night
Was my heart in me
Now beholden to me
No longer golden in me

ONE HUNDRED NINETY NINE

When within a heart doubt does seep
Should the love
No longer keep
As the clouds before the storm
If one be observant
They are forewarn
Yet to ourselves do we lie
In hopes that love does not dwindle
And die
As an ash
From fire leapt
To fall to ground
With brightness kept
Does it alight anew
Or smolder and die
With no fuel to fuel
And so to ourselves do we lie
In hopes that love
Does not dwindle and die

TWO HUNDRED TWO

My love, once fiery and bold
Has grown weary
And smolders cold
For the fuel it needs to subsist
Of one, it does seem to consist
Yet hope I still place
In this love which I dream not commonplace
Even as a shadow encircle and clench
And my mind, with doubt now drench
For this heart does resist and strain
Against the mind
Which shackles and reigns
For this heart upon my sleeve I wear
My mind does know, of love, of two must conceive
And through your actions, to my heart, do relieve
My mind does know the assumption I take them to be
And so the flames, myself, I seem to fan
Yet grown weary my strength does wan
And my tongue I do try to hold
For I wish not to sway
For truth in love should not be mold as clay
Yet hope still play
That in your heart
This love still lay

TWO HUNDRED FOUR

One is as a pond
Filled with the water of life's experiences
One cannot control the amount of flowing
One cannot control when
One is as the the pond in seasons
During times the water is low
During times the water is high
Sometimes the surface calm and placid
Sometimes the surface is disturbed
For even the smallest droplets
Create ripples upon the surface

TWO HUNDRED FIVE

In love the world is filled with blissful delights
And the nights are guarded with gilded stars
For sorrow holds no place
In love's sweet face
And days and nights do converge as one
Only through itself undone
And when love no longer come
And sorrow's face does take it's place
The world is filled with sullen nights
Guarded with blackened bars
Askew'ing the light
From love's gilded stars

TWO HUNDRED NINE

When you called for me
When you looked at me
Only love is what I saw
I trusted in you
And you trusted in me
When I left I knew you were there
And when I left I knew you were scared
But you believed in me
And when I looked at you
I saw only love in your eyes
Because you knew love is all I felt for you to
You let me fly
Knowing I would never leave you
And I would never hurt you
Because when you looked at me
Love is all you saw in my eyes
Respectfully you let me fly
Trusting in me
Trusting in you
For all eternity

TWO HUNDRED TWENTY ONE

A nobler love so fair
It's strength to me please lend
So as the oak
I shall not bend
Even for lust's boisterous air
And on the road we all do travel
Sometimes we stumble and sway
As love's riddle we try to unravel
And mold
As if from simple clay
Yet a nobler love so fair
It's strength to me does lend
For in it's hope there is no compare
To give me the heart
So it's name I can defend
And to one day
Upon love's breast
It too
Shall find my rest

TWO HUNDRED TWENTY SIX

We esteem for greater in love
Do we break the surface
Only to see our folly
Then in regret we run
Saying it was not to be
Loathsome of ourselves
Disassociated
Accusing others
Of what we are guilty of
Scared of the reflection
Saying it was not to be

TWO HUNDRED THIRTY TWO

Life is full of many mountains and valleys
Through which we make our journey
And the road we choose
Is the road of our choosing
And the consequences we suffer upon the road
Are from the road we chose
As the winds do blow
Sometimes heavy
And sometimes soft and low
Even if the winds blow hard
And we stray from path
It is our choosing to pursue
And not stay to wait the passing of the storm
For when the sky is dark
And the road unsure
It is our choosing to pursue
Headlong and stubborn
With heavy foot
Upon treacherous course
Yet sometimes through the storm we must go
If only to learn
That which we truly yearn
And the consequences we suffer
Are the consequences of the road we chose
And sometimes we win
And sometimes we lose

TWO HUNDRED THIRTY SIX

My heart
I hold to you
And my hands cannot contain
All that remains
For in my hands it lay
Crumbled and dust
And through my fingers I must let it pass
And the winds blow the pieces
Like dust on the windswept plain
I offer it to you
For I no longer have need
And it's call I no longer can heed
And from the dust
I lay at your feet
And the tears I shed
While still I can weep
I hope to fertilize your soul
And you can spring forth
Like the flowers which in spring do bud
And to the sun you can stretch in all your glory
For this love
I feel I only rent
For the owner has gone away
Too him
Your love still stay

TWO HUNDRED FORTY ONE

We dream of beauty
And all it's qualities
Of it's refinement and it's unity
It's universality
But when faced with it
We close ourselves
In it's shining light
We see only our differences
Our inequality
And the thing which that we revere
We soon become to hate
We seek only to mar it
And bring it down to our level
We do not wish to ascend to it's level
Only to bring the level down
To make it easier to achieve
We must learn to accept our frailties and differences
And once we recognize them
To change what we can
And accept what we cannot
Only then can we achieve the level of beauty
For we fool ourselves in thinking
That by lowering ourselves we achieve the same
In our achievement we lose sight of the fact
That our achievement is lower

TWO HUNDRED FORTY TWO

Two hearts collide
And in a shower of sparks
They are joined
And when they part
What does fill the lost part
Is one strong enough to hold
To hold the new found mend
For one cannot ascertain
Until one is deep within the rend
In hopes they are one
Who can mend

TWO HUNDRED FORTY SIX

Experiences form perceptions
Perceptions form experiences
The shores shape the seas
The seas shape the shores
The wanderer
Detached
Unaffected
Only more attached then is known
What binds him
Frees him
What frees him
Binds him

TWO HUNDRED FORTY EIGHT

In our heads
What dreams do we keep
Which mask is it
That we do seek
For many are worn
To play our parts
What lies behind
Unknown
What lies beneath
The mask beguiles the dream
The dream beguiles the mask
For the rain feeds the river
And the river feeds the rain
In which mask do we dream
And which dream do we mask

TWO HUNDRED FIFTY

The beauty of the setting sun
Burning in your eyes
So sad
So forlorn
Upon wings we were once borne
Upon the ground we now tread
Shackled in weight of dread
The beauty of the setting sun
Reminding of what was promised
Of what was said
Burning in our eyes
What was gained
What was lost
Soaring
The miles in flight
Trudging
The agony of time
The aching of muscles
Remembrances of the effortlessness
Upon the wing which we were born
The beauty of the setting sun

TWO HUNDRED FIFTY FOUR

Only the good die young
For innocence is lost in age
With age comes reality
A reality we suffer
And complain
Yet reality is what we make it
In us we have the power
To change it
But it is much easier
To sit and complain
For only the good die young

TWO HUNDRED FIFTY SEVEN

Fill your cup and raise your glass
To forget your woes
And soon let your troubles pass
And let your heart no longer be surrounded
By sorrows now passed
Drain your glass to nothing drop
And let your spirits free
To fly atop
And come to realize you are not the last
Nor the first
To feel love's darts
And let these feelings pass
For your seriousness does worry me
So quench these fires
Which in your soul amass
And to you my friend
I now raise my glass
And say to you
Please empty your soul
And let it's troubles pass
For you are not the first
Nor the last
To feel love's sting
As it pass
And compare your soul
To that from which you drink
If it be full
No more can fill
And overflow it will
Upon the brink
So empty your glass
And to love let us toast
As we fill our cups
So our hearts may soon boast

TWO HUNDRED SIXTY ONE

When these fires within me do wane
No longer stoked by the muses who fan them
And still and quiet
As a sleepy silent fog
Do now reign
Where then
Shall I wander
For the fires within
Were as the beacon light of some lighthouse kept
Now my guide is gone
With no light to see
Which way is land
And which way lie the seas
For now unchained from the guiding light
liberated
My course is left to me
Unfettered
Now out to sea
Or upon the rocks and away with me

TWO HUNDRED SIXTY NINE

For the soul of an artist is made of coal
To feed the hungry fires
Of creativities need
And this we must learn to parcel
So as not to ourselves become consumed
By the fires in which we feed

TWO HUNDRED SEVENTY NINE

Seeking attention
Using it as control
Seemingly powerful
Using for an escape
From oneself
To lose oneself
A smiling angel
With golden songs
To soothe the pain
Devil with horn's worn low
Only building up
To keep low
A devil made angel
Or an angel made devil
By temptation's free and innocent song
Only now where does the heart belong
When angel's are devils
And devil's are angels
In a massed confused throng
As only an instrument
Played by hands
Oh
The complexities to which we are thrown

TWO HUNDRED EIGHTY

Your heart, I did hope to posses
As something I could call my own
And bathe in your beauties light
As the sun at dawn
And when the moon is high
To be warmed by your heart
And your body
As the warmest blanket upon the bed
But now I feel, your heart, to me, is not to be
For the heart I hold
In grasped hand
Is not free
And a love I know that which is not free
To sing as the sweetest bird perched upon any tree
Is not a love I wish to own
Nor call my own
As the grape upon the vine
When squeezed, to make the sweetest wine
So to is your heart to me
Likened to a clutching child
Clutching a loved toy in fear
In fear it will be lost
So to am I
Clutching your heart
And in my embrace
Your heart is not allowed to race
Only to become smothered
As the flame with no air to feed
And this love I hoped would grow
Now I must, myself, throw
For I squeezed your heart dry
And you are no longer able to fly
Nor a tear from your eye, to fall
No tears of sadness, nor tears of joy

For the well from which they be sprung
Is wrung dry
And no feeling left to cry
And no blame shall I place upon thee
For all the blame I take unto me
For your heart, I did find upon the ground
And with no thought to who it may belong
I thanked the heavens, for this small grace
But now I must let you go
For me, your heart will never glow
And from your eyes, it's light will never show
And all I seek, is your souls forgiveness
For the havoc I did wreak
For the heart you gave, belonged to another
With not enough time to recover
And the heart you gave, was not meant for me
For it was not free
And the door was still locked
Even as I knocked
And I am not let in
As your heart is locked

TWO HUNDRED EIGHTY SEVEN

When my skies grow dark and grim
To you is to whom I turn
Yet I know this song which I sing
This scorned hymn
Which my heart begin
Shall fall upon your ears
And to me your strength shall lend
As I know this day is not the end
When my skies grow dark and grim
and the night does ever last
This sorrowed hymn
From my breast begin
And innocence I know I cannot claim
For we all are not free from love's sin
So open my heart
Which in weakness lay
To find the strength for another day
And thank you I must
In this gift within
As I know this is not the end
And soon my heart shall play
In your radiant ray
For we are not free
Some cost we must pay
And though scorned now I feel
I cannot forget love's sweet peal
And in your radiant ray
My heart, again shall play

TWO HUNDRED NINETY TWO

What do we lose when our hearts bleed
What do we lose from our hearts needs
When the tides are low
What do we do with love
It's song no longer new
What shall we seek to take it's place
Will the promise be held
Or soon break
Out with the old and in with the new
A simple proclamation to shore a weak foundation
What was held
To deny the true
But happiness only lies
When it is left to aesthetics to decide
In it's guise now hide
As love is blind
And often unkind
For at first is simple play
Yet the journey is long
Many obstacles will meet
And all is not flowers and sweet
And though tween two a connection made
It only takes one to cause to fade
For when time does wipe away
What is left is what time cannot steal away
With promise held
A torch through darkness lead way

JUSTIFICATION (TWO HUNDRED NINETY FOUR)

Our dreams
We in reality ourselves kill
For we go in blind
And surface wide eyed
And now stained
Our hearts
We no longer feel
Our dreams now dust
Now settle in lust
How lofty our goals once were
Now blinded as they turn to rust
Indulged, we search for more
Saying to the wise
"You are old"
In righteousness we are now bold
And in the future
We use our past to amuse
And the present we save for another day
Forgetting all we touch
Does leave a keepsake
And when we repent
We forget the golden rule
For our past is past
For hopes of the new
And the dreams we hold
We say only an ideal
Something unattainable
Only a goal which is unreachable
If but only it could be real
So our dreams we turn to rust
For later we can always repent
And a new temple erect

TWO HUNDRED NINETY FIVE

The ambitious shall lead us
Only the leaders are followers unbeknownst
For the prize they seek is basic
Man's need to be powerful and respected
To hide our faults through greatness
To exclaim it is our right
And our proclamation

TWO HUNDRED NINETY SIX

In our ambitions we feel justified
Justified for what we take
Because of what we gave
And through our ambitions now hide
And we exclaim
We are not accountable for misdeeds done
Because of what to the table we bring
For man has many faults and high ideals
And this no man can overcome
Even I must succumb
Yet we all lay scorn upon some
Whilst others do same
And upon their heads we lay no blame
For some we see as human
And others we see as less
Unable to be blinded by their weak light
For differences in thought and action
Do make up the human caste
But we hide ourselves behind ideals
And lay blame to others
To explain our wrong way
And then fall back to our humanness and proclaim
"We are only human!"
To away ourselves from blame

TWO HUNDRED NINETY SEVEN

Is love blind,
Or is it the fear of loneliness which causes us to be blind?

THREE HUNDRED FOUR

The greatest gift you see
Is the lover to the beloved
And the beloved to the lover
For without the one
The other
As yet unknown
It's beauty
Remains undiscovered
Like a radiant light when found
It's embers stirred to life
So now to show with new found life
What ounce burned low

THREE HUNDRED TEN

A simple fool
Ruling a place of dreams
See how he weeps
His tears a darkened ink
See how he laughs
Echoing these empty halls
His flight first here
Then there
A madman in mocked majesty
His crown of brightly polished brass
His clothes in stateliness clash
See how he plays
Ruling a place of dreams
A child's land
See how he weeps
A marionette
To a child's hand

THREE HUNDRED TWELVE

How much are we ourselves to blame
How much are we the cause to in our reactions
How little do we want to know
In the seeds with which we do sew
Innocence we claim
For sympathy will then be our fame
Risen above ourselves
Above our troubles
So soon we forget
In all that we beset
It's easier to lie to ourselves
When we lie with someone who doesn't care
How much of this hole
Do we dig ourselves
If only we would learn how to put down the spade
And see what our hands have made

THREE HUNDRED TWENTY

On these wings which carry me
Carry me into the light
Deeper shall I go
Deeper into this enveloping night
Discovering what is known
Discovering what is shown
Another day is new
Another day is gone
Another day shall be added to this pack
From which we wish we could be free
Innocence is what we seek
Forgiveness is what we hope for
Freedom from ourselves in all that we have done
Living without regret
Upon these wings which carry us
Carry us into the light
Soaring into the darkness of this place within us
You say that I am already lost
And I shall say that I am only who I am
I hope that you will not leave me
As I know that you cannot stay
If only there was an easier way
But I can only be who I am
And place no blame on you
Deadened by my own hand
See me as I am
This war that rages within me
Within me is where I must stand
So trust in me as I have trust in nothing
Felled by my own hand
On these wings which carry me
Carry me into the light
Deeper into this darkened night
Awakening to see you in the coming light

THREE HUNDRED TWENTY SIX

With the dawning of the day, comes another day
Another day I sit
I sit and wait alone
The brightness of the sun
In which this pain no longer can hide
To her I wish I could run
But air is all that is there
Am I to heavy for you
Perhaps I came on to strong
But all this pain with which I feel
Has turned to joy when I think of you
With the dawning of the day, comes another day
Another day I sit
I sit and wait alone
You say I left you
Even though I sit by you
But what can I say
I cannot change myself
As in myself I roam
So here I sit
Alone I fear I shall stay
With myself again to blame
For you I could not entertain
And this love within me
Again shall turn to pain
So when you see me
Please do not look and stare
And remind me
Of all this pain inside me
And why I sit alone and wait
In the hope that someday
Someday she will sit beside me

THE ANVIL (THREE HUNDRED THIRTY ONE)

This sadness, I let wash over me
This pain I walk into
We are forged upon experience's anvil
We are beaten by his hammer
We are shaped by life's eye
We are shaped by ourselves
In passion to be cooled
In passion can be fooled
In fear we wall ourselves
Against that which we need
We self-destruct
That which we wish to build
This sadness, please do temper me
So I can see the world
So I can live with this world
This pain do harden me
So I do not break when the hammer falls
So I can fight my way to you
Give me the strength to find you
Give me the strength to hold you
Have faith in me
When I have not the faith in myself
Hold me up when I cannot stand
So these walls which we build
We can turn to dust
Before our hearts
Before our hearts turn to rust
And fade away
And this sadness washes our hearts away
So we can live with ourselves
Until the day we break our walls away
And the light does wash it all away

THREE HUNDRED THIRTY THREE

I don't understand you
You are lonely
Yet, here you sit in solitude
Why not go out and try to find someone
And if it's only for right now
Then right now it is
Because I've been right then
And now
Here I sit
Alone
With the memories of then
Let it go they said
But how can I
For then I will fall
Fall down again
And how many times have I fallen
How many times have I been broken
How many times must I mend
You say you don't understand me
But here I stand before you
If you could only look through
My eyes
Then you might realize
Then you might see me
And no longer judge me in the way
My time, I spend
As everyone wants someone
But for different ways
And for different reasons
And everyone tries to find someone
In different ways
And different reasons
And I don't want to lose myself
In someone

I don't want to lose myself
I just found myself
And I am not that bad
If only you would let me be who I am
Then you will understand me
Only then will you understand me
And then you will see why
Why I do not run and hide
From myself
Why would I lose myself
Only to find myself
Only to find myself
In the end
And why would I lie to myself
Only to find myself
When I want to lose myself
Lose myself with someone
And they can lose themselves with me
So together
We can find ourselves again
Till the day
The day when we die

THIRTY HUNDRED THIRTY NINE

I had finally moved on
Why do you come back to haunt me
Why do you taunt me
Do you like to see my pain
Do you even see my pain
And you wonder why it's goodbye
I no longer can take the abuse
I no longer can take the excuse
I don't want to keep playing this game
So why do you haunt me
Why do you taunt me
You say your sorry
You say you didn't know
But then you always have an excuse
Something to blame
But don't we all in this silly game
You walked out
You walked back in
What did you think was going to happen
It's always the same
Why do you still haunt me
Why do you still taunt me
Why does all this love turn to hate
Is this destiny
Is this fate
Why do you still haunt me
Why do you still taunt me
I had finally moved on
And you can't look at me

THREE HUNDRED FORTY ONE

What is this inside me that drives me
This aspiration within me
For I am only a man, nothing heavenly
Does this solitude within me, build me
Or only destroy me, slowly
All this pain, all this anguish
All this happiness within me
I ask myself what I am, what drives me
Alone in all my searching
This bitterness fuels me
This passion ignites me
I ask you to show me the answers
And you show me myself
I ask you what I have done to deserve this
And you show me myself
As I am only a man, nothing heavenly
Only who I am, only what I am
You say I have lost myself, to myself
And I can say that I am only that which I am
Only a man
I have no answers
I have only questions
Like all before me
Like all after me
Is this a curse within me
Damnation
For I am only a man
Nothing heavenly
Choosing to find myself within myself
Choosing to find the answers

Within myself
As a man only can
And what awaits me
Scares me
As I am only a man, nothing heavenly
And my despair I must embrace
This solitude
To find what it is inside me
That drives me

THREE HUNDRED FORTY THREE

Upon this paper I write my soul to me
My thoughts to me
What else have I to do
Sometimes in happiness
Sometimes in sadness
This sorrow and joy
What is it to me when all is lost to me
A beginning with no end
The journey is long
Sometimes cold, sometimes hot
Hidden in the mysteries lies only mysteries
Unbearable at times
And delivered from at times
Who would follow me and who would lead me
In this place
As no one knows this place
Not even I
I who live in this place
I have tried to run from here
Only to return to this place
Because a fools race it is when one tries to hasten from themselves
A losing race
If only I had the grace
How little I know
What have I lost
What have I found
Alone in this place
So upon this paper I write my soul to me
My thoughts to me

THREE HUNDRED FORTY FIVE

When I look at you
Look at the way you light up
The way your smile spreads across your lips
At the way you walk so carelessly
And how I wish it was me
Who caused you to be this way
How many times have I wanted to grab hold of you
And kiss your pain away
To look in your eyes and see
And see that you trusted in me
And see your pain washed away
To hold your hand so effortlessly
To hold you tight
And keep you warm at night
And how I wish
How I wish it could be me
But I am nothing
Like all the rest
Just second best
And how I wish I could be something
The sun, the moon, and the stars to you
But I am nothing
Dreaming of something
Like all the rest
I wish you could see
I wish you could understand
This dream in me
But I have not told you
I choked, you left
You saw it in my eyes and ran away

As I am nothing
Like all the rest
Hoping for a day
When love will stay
And how much of you is me, like all of us
And from nothing you gave me
You gave me something
This dream of someday finding something
Like all of us

THREE HUNDRED FORTY SIX

You looked for me
And you could not find me from among all the twists and turns
As I had sat down to rest
Weary, from searching for you
And as I slumbered, peacefully dreaming
You did not notice me, and walked on by
So many distractions
So much to pass the time with
So much to taste
To appease ourselves with and cause sate
As upon my head father time had crowned me
With flecks of grey, flecks of gold
While I slept
So you did not notice me
And upon my face was graveness worn, time worn
Though rested from the many miles tread with somberness
Lost within reflection
I looked for you and walked as passer by
For I had not noticed you
Lost in soliloquy with the muses in my head
As to what I would say
When I finally found you
Only to become a statue to you
With nothing said
As solitude as my dark cloaked companion
I still look for you
While the other so gayly play
I search for you
Hoping it not be in vain
Until the day I may rest with you
A soft smile across my face shall then play

THREE HUNDRED FORTY SEVEN

"Come, come and join us.", they said with a hearty warm grasp of the shoulder.

"I am,", he said, with a devilishly shy smile.

"You are but so quiet.", they said "Let yourself relax and not be so serious and somber."

"Let your troubles and thought pass, and come share a drink with us and stay a while."

"I will stay and relax with you," he said, "but as to my thoughts and troubles, they will stay, of no account to me."

"But," they said, "have a drink, if only to wash them away." "And so then to let yourself free of them, if only briefly."

"Briefly, yes." he said, "As the cloud, which obscuring the sun and hiding it's rays of light so that we can no longer see it, we know it does still be."

"For the sun, we know, does still remain in its heavenly and lofty place, as it is only the cloud that secrets it away and the cloud will pass to reveal the sun shortly."

"My friend," they said, "you do need a drink!"

"No, he said, "but thank you for the offer as I can see that you only wish the best for me, and no harm."

"So then come and join us, as you seem to need a break from yourself." they said.

"No, but thank you again for the offer, and I wish to cause no harm." he said.

"Well," they said, "some alarm is raised of course, as we do not like to see you this way for it does not seem you are yourself."

"Thank you for the kind words." he said, "And do not worry over me or my words because I am indeed myself."

"Well then, will you not stay?" they said.

"I wish I could." he said, "But my fires have been stoked, and as much as I tried, I feel, I would only bring heaviness upon you and your happiness here."

"But only a small drink," they said, "to cool the fires within you as you said."

"Nay my friend." he said, "But you make it hard to resist."

"Then stay." they said, with broad smiles and bemoaned looks. "Do not resist us."

"I must." he said. "As I have chosen a different way then you, but please do not misinterpret me and allow my words to misrepresent me."

"No," they said, "we do not misinterpret you and we understand."

"Good luck to you, and remember you are welcome here always." they said.

"And good luck to you." he said, "And I will not forget you, or to visit again."

"Till we meet again then." they said.

"Yes, till we meet again then." he said.

THREE HUNDRED FIFTY TWO

"Your words you say are beautiful and within me cause to stir feelings of such love and hope."

"Your kindness to me is appreciated."

"But such radiant words your soul does speak and why is your countenance so sad? Do you not feel these things of which you speak?"

"No, I feel them all the more. My countenance would reflect the reality of contrariness of this place in which we live. As the words are comforting to me, for from me they do spring. I grow tired and weak of defending myself from influences both of this society and of myself."

"But do you not find solace in yourself since you say these things are from you sprung?"

"Yes and both no."

"So you are a hypocrite then? As how can one be of both when they are opposite."

"These words I speak are dream like in that the reality tends to be opposite."

"How do you mean dream like?"

"Well, I mean dream like in the sense that, yes, they are moving but we wake up to the reality and forget our dreams as they are difficult to obtain so we prefer to sleep and dream then to work to make them true."

"I see, then how does society come in to play?"

"Society, or I should rather have said external influences do control us through acceptance."

"Society or external influences?"

"External influences I should rather say as external influences manifests itself as society which is a blanket statement to include both individual and group influence. And a hypocrite I feel as I tire of defending myself from voices both internal and external."

"You say internal as well as external?"

"Yes."

"That is hypocritical?"

"Yes, and I will try to explain the juxtaposition if I am capable enough."

"Surely."

"I say tired and weak as one would compare themselves to a runner who when finished running the allotted space just a little further is added, then added again, and so on and so forth."

"I see."

"And this goes on indefinitely until the runner tires and feels they can go on no further. Yet again they must continue."

"I see, but how does this correlate with society, or as you prefer, external influences?"

"Let me try another way"

"Okay."

"A sleeper awakes, and is filled with fondness of the recollection of dream. And in their excitement they begin to share their dreams with others. Who in their turn scoff and tease them because they are not of the understanding or of the desire of understanding. So after a time the one who dreams begins to feel the resentment and ridicule their visions suffer them and begin to resent themselves and their dreams as they believe they must be wrong because so many are against them. So they begin to follow the many because it is easier and far less lonely and considered saner."

"Saner?"

"Yes."

"How do you mean?"

"Sane in the sense that when one goes against society to protect and/or serve themselves they are outcast and considered weird, antisocial, strange, or whatever word is used to describe them to others, they are different. And the turmoil this brings about inside the person outcast can manifest itself in many ways. You must hear my words subjectively rather then objectively as I am limited and I must apologize for my pedestrian."

"No apology necessary, and I will try to follow."

"Thank you, now where was I?"

"I believe you were saying something about a sleeper or dreamer who awakens and then shares their dream with an unsympathetic and understanding society."

"Oh yes, now I remember. So the person awakens another self to overrule the other self. To cause to sleep what was awakened. And this duality causes strife in that the one resists the other which takes place within one. One side counteracts the other resulting in hypocritical thoughts and actions depending in which side rules at the moment. So if one wishes to go against all they risk much. And if one goes against themselves they risk all."

"So you are stating that external influences can guide and direct as well as internal influences?"

"Yes. and that the external can begin to guide and direct the internal unnoticed so one feels it is their own direction and are uninfluenced by outside influences."

"I see. How doe one remain true to themselves?"

"They must believe in themselves. They must have the wisdom, patience, and the desire to see and accept the truth. To have the ability to find the truth in however it is guised as the truth can be a comforting shimmer or a blinding harsh light. My sadness comes from the rejection of myself from myself. From the views of the external which becomes the internal. How happy would we not be if we were not subject to the judgements of others. How much of these judgements do we begin to internalize and make our own. That is why I am sad. Because my dreams are being stripped of me by my own hand, just as the other hand catches them and brings them to me. The thing which frees me also pains me and imprisons me within its walls."

"I see. And I am glad that I am not you my friend." said with a smile.

"So to am I (laughs and smiles). We are not to confuse external and internal influences, as they do influence each other. We must not blame the external so to avoid the internal and vice versa. We must not confuse the one with the other to avert the consequences of actions taken by either. This also requires great perseverance of which we are hesitant to pursue as the truth can be hurtful."

"You think much I would think."

"Always my friend, you should feel lucky."

"I do (smiling)"

"Is my explanation sufficient?"

"Yes, I do believe it is. Although you have raised other questions while you answered some."

"Another time for those."

"Thank you."

THREE HUNDRED SIXTY FOUR

Clouded in shadow and mists, swirling and mingling
Ever changing, a picture hanging
The vision before us played upon by judgements fancy
This dream beheld before us
Upon what wings does it fly before us
In darkness or in light
In heft of gold or heft of lead
Of earth below or sky above
What fuel do the fires that alight feed
This picture dreamed before us
How shall we construe the images seen
Do we interpret it or it interpret us
A reflection of what we can only see in seconds
Can we truly perceive
Or to us does it deceive
Can we trust in us
In the vision that we see
Do we accurately conceive
Are we strong enough to delve into
To suffer the fires that burn
To see the picture hanging for that which it be
Amid the shadows and mists swirling and mingling
Ever changing
For that which it truly be

THREE HUNDRED SEVENTY ONE

You ask of me to cross this sea
And you will wait for me
Alone
As I shall be with your promise
As my ship
And your heart as my sail
I cast away my lines
To you, to this place
The kisses you blow are as the wind within my sails
Filling them, and me
With what they, and I, both need to leave this place
And your side
Oh, the power of these seas
Their might
Oh, the power of these winds
Their irresistible force
Long I battled the seas and winds
In defiance proud
Even when I trembled to my very core
This torch I carried I let it not be extinguished
Through these storms of which assailed me
As love, even in it's bitterest hour, cannot be stripped of it's beauty
Nor it's light smothered
Only covered
Yet underneath it still does shine
And the seas finally grew calm
And the winds grew weary of their torrent and silenced
Upon placid seas I sailed with silence
With struggle gone
I grew weary and longed for you
And found comfort in the present with the past
And the dream of the future
And the future came to me as if out of the sea
So distant, and now, so near

And upon her shores I anchored my hope to tether me
Until my return, and you with me
And these seas and these winds I now befriend
As they are known to me
And they do carry me
Of you with me
So come, oh you angry sea
With all your ferocity
Come and show your teeth to me
And to you, howling winds, come hither also and show me your torrent
For I know with your tempestuous show
You only hasten me in my journey
Thus filled I again set sail
Set sail to your shores

THREE HUNDRED SEVENTY NINE

O winged glory, to such heights you ascend
On winds which make others bend
Soaring so mightily, so triumphantly
That naught you hear from winds pass roaring
Turning and twisting, eluding at every pass
With twinkle in eye that sparkles as glass
Ever closer you circle
Ever near you come
As a whisper softly spoken
Then to turn and run
Carried by the winds
Lost in their rustling begun
And with each going the chase begins anew
Your smile so sweetly beckoning
Or a farewell adieu

THREE HUNDRED EIGHTY THREE

Again I face these thoughts within me
And I wonder where they will lead me
So much I see
And yet so much is veiled to me
I have come so far
And now I can not turn back
As my footsteps have been lost to the windswept sands in this place
I can only go on
By this that guides me
Have I chosen right in that which leads me
Or is it only weakness born of this burden
Am I strong enough to carry this given to me
Again I face these thoughts within me
These burning questions that do forge me
When upon the anvil I am lain
Shaped by the hammer that falls

THREE HUNDRED EIGHTY FOUR

Acceptance, conformity
Our base human desires to conquer and relent
Our "will to power"
Some regress while others pass
What lies behind the mask worn
The gentle smile
The stern frown
Forgiveness for the freedom won
Awarded in the artless aspiration of a design forever changing
Liberation sought from the self made manacles of entitlement
Seen as only entertainment
A mere "nothing"
Beauty smeared by lust's lewdness
In a moment when passions fires alight and roar
Oh, how the feeling does make one soar
Pains forgotten
Seeming aged old lore
Faded now
As a word long spoken
Floating above and beyond
To and fro
Carried by inspirations waves as heat from the flame
In a moment remembered
In the twinkle of an eye
In a twinkle forgotten
In a moment of time
But nature makes her laws forever wending
Fanning the flames on higher
Till the source be spent
Fanning the ashes
Till the life be sent

THREE HUNDRED EIGHTY SIX

Born in pain
A pain which bored straight through
Awakening what lied deep inside
Regret holds the door
That redemption tries to close
We make our choices
Of what we hold onto and what we let go
Can you see this pain
Can you understand this
Of why I do this
Of why I have made this choice
To stay here
I know it is not for you
As I know my words shall fail me
And it rips me apart and weighs down on me
I only wish that I have the strength
To see this through
To not let it go
As I know someday this will end
This pain and anger in me
That burn in me
I can no longer hide and turn away
I only wish that you can understand me
We make our choices of what we hold on to
And what we let go
Regret holds the door
That redemption tries to close

THREE HUNDRED EIGHTY SEVEN

Tomorrow holds the promise of salvation
That whispers upon the winds of today

THREE HUNDRED EIGHTY EIGHT

Cast away, suffering these winds that torment me
A drift in this sea
By my own design or is it destiny
How long will I stay here
Ruminating
How long before I lose this weight in me
I once sailed so effortlessly across these seas
When did I lose sight
I was once so happy no doubt could turn me
No longer can I turn so easily
Nor do I ask of your pity
As I have no pity for myself
For you do not see what I see
You do not feel what I feel
Cast away and set adrift
Like so many others of ages past
And yet to come
Though time endured
I must carry on
I must keep seeking
As the dawning sun awakens life
May it still awaken in me the possibility
That I have the strength
To reach that which I seek

THREE HUNDRED NINETY EIGHT

The assumption of the presumption of the first thought
The book read before the pages upend
So sure of our perspective
Judge and jury
With no time for deliberations
For fools they be who are not to our thought receptive
Fact and fiction fall before pretext
A self conscious guise to feeling
Where ego stands
Right and wrong crumble

FOUR HUNDRED TWO

You tell me to switch gears and forget my fears
While your heart I know to him, still sway
You tell me to switch gears and let not fall my tears
While to him you still stray
How many times will I fall for this game
How many times will I, the endings always the same
That subtle spark in your eye
The coy thrust of your chest
I've always known their little lies
The endings always the same
How many times will I fall for this game
You say you could not tell that for you my feelings fell
But then why would you
While for him your heart swayed
And here I am again
My heart fell preyed
How many times must I fall
Fall for this game
The endings always the same
I wanted your eyes to sparkle for me
I wanted to alight in your heart a fire
A fire for me
But to him your heart still swayed
Was it to cause him pain
To feel a little hurt
To prove a point
Gone before the start
I played again this part
And the endings always the same

FOUR HUNDRED FOUR

To heaven and to hell
Holds not the compel
For one can only comply
To the heart and soul
Which within their breast does lie
For God in heaven
And God in hell
Do know what we do not yet tell
For our hearts and souls
Do their trueness show
As easily seen
As the suns brightness glow
For we cannot hide our intent
Even if one recompent

FOUR HUNDRED SEVEN

Every moment that passes
Is another moment without you
You ask me to wait for you
When you were never here
Another season comes and goes
Alone again I look for you
Is this dream just a dream
Just smoke, distracting me, choking me
Alone I feel the currents against me
Am I just drifting in a moment
I reach for your hand
And all I see is mine
Alone again I look for you
I will not let this dream choke me
I will not let this darkness blind me
And this emptiness in me I will not let consume me
Though these memories are memories without you
And the moments that pass pass without you
They bring me closer to you
And I am thankful for the pain
The pain that alights the fires in me
That drive me
That consume me
And bring me closer to you

FEAR (FOUR HUNDRED EIGHT)

When this hope dies
And the fire burns itself to ashes
Blown away by the winds of time
Blowing away what was left of me
It's so dark here now
Without the fires to light me
It's so cold here now
Without the fires to warm me
These embers in me grow cold
Awaiting your love to blow through me
Awakening them from their slumber
And in my eyes do you see the loneliness
Do you see the darkness there now
What powerlessness I hold over this
In time these wings will mend
And again support me
In time the fires will ignite in me
Smoldering now
Let me rebuild from me
From these ashes of me
Let time blow away the dust from me
Let time give me the time
To find the strength in me
Breaking myself down
So that I can rise from these ruins
Let time's cold winds numb this pain
Till these scars heal
I shall embrace this solitude in me
To find the strength within myself
To overcome myself
And find my way to you

MY LOVE(FOUR HUNDRED NINE)

My love
We've waited so long for this
Endured so many sleepless nights wondering
Wondering when our time would come
So many lonely nights
Alone with our fears
Protecting ourselves with it's coldness
Numbing us
I've no regrets on what we've done
I've no regrets on what we've become
Only here matters now
The only thing that matters now is us
My love
We've waited so long for this
Open our eyes so we can see that we're not dreaming
The roads been long
And is longer yet still
But it's lead us here
My love
Take my hand and let us see where it takes us
Let us leave behind our fears
Which hold us here
My love
Take my hand and let's free ourselves
To take these steps together
My love

DREAMS (FOUR HUNDRED TEN)

How many times have I wandered here
Wandered these roads searching
Searching for the answers to my dreams
My dreams of you
How many times will I fly
Only to fall
Broken
How many storms must I endure
Till the rains wash this pain away
Wash this loneliness away
Leaving the better me
Leaving the dream in me
Let me cast away this weight
So that I can breath
And fuel the fire in me
Give me the strength to follow my convictions
To pick myself up again
And raise my eyes to the horizon
And take the steps again
Wandering these roads searching
Searching for the answers to my dreams
The dreams in me
My dreams of you

WHAT TOMORROW MAY BRING
(FOUR HUNDRED ELEVEN)

Are we strong enough
Strong enough to see through ourselves
To truly see what lies inside
So we can read ourselves
And see what we truly want
What we truly need
To recognize what we deserve
And see what we create with our own hands
Despite ourselves
Despite our desires
Are we strong enough to remember
To remember what part we play
In what we choose to change us
To shape us
Are we strong enough to follow what we set
To follow through to the end
To follow through to a beginning
To open ourselves
And give ourselves despite our fears
To see through our tears of joy
As well as sorrow
And see the light dawning from tomorrow
So we can unlock our hearts
And tear them apart
Then gather the pieces
To tear down the walls
To reach out from the shadows in ourselves
To begin a new start
Embracing what tomorrow may bring

WALLS(FOUR HUNDRED TWELVE)

Hardened in the fires of this pain
Tempered in the lonely solitude
Only to be broken by your promise

These walls we've built to protect us
Appear so strong
We fool ourselves
Hoping we are wrong
We hide from ourselves
Hoping we aren't wrong

So we do not have to see
Blinding ourselves
Remembering what we want
And neglecting the rest
Killing ourselves so we can breath
But in the end we find ourselves still here
No movement forward
Only backward

These walls we've built to protect us
Appear so strong
We fool ourselves
Hoping we are wrong
We hide from ourselves
Hoping we aren't wrong

Till we bury ourselves deep inside
Within the shadows deepest corners to hide
Will we hear the call
Will we see the light when it comes
Can we escape the hole we've dug
Escape ourselves
To allow ourselves to finally breath

These walls we've built to protect us
Appear so strong
We fool ourselves
Hoping we are wrong
We hide from ourselves
Hoping we aren't wrong

BARS (FOUR HUNDRED FOURTEEN)

We believe our dream that we hold so dear
We see what could be
We believe what is promised
Overlooking what is
Then claim the victim when it all falls apart
How many mistakes we make until we become numb
Saying never again
Only to fall below the surface again
Fighting for air to breath
We reach out
To pull ourselves out
And take the first breath
Cleansing ourselves of the pain
Falling away
Forgetting the pain and sorrow with each breath
Can we forgive ourselves
In time only to forget
Only to fall below the surface again
In time will heal
Only leaving scars
Will we remember
Remember the reasons
And not allow them to become our bars

FOUR HUNDRED FIFTEEN

Toying with the fantasy
What promise it shall bring
Losing oneself in it's heady swirl
Realizing to late
At what cost they bring
Unable to reconcile
Beginning again
Lashing out
No sense of control
Feed the fire inside
Burning brighter
Getting hungrier
Beginning again
Becoming an addiction
Sacrificing oneself to the self indulgent flames
While saying never again
Maybe just this one more time
How many times must we blind ourselves
Before we see
How many times will we burn ourselves
Before we find ourselves
When will we close our eyes
So we can see the light
When will we believe in ourselves
And free ourselves
From the doubt in us
The fear
From beginning again
Are we afraid of losing a reason to blame
A reason to explain
This sacrifice
Beginning again

FOUR HUNDRED SIXTEEN

Afraid of letting go of what you know
Afraid of letting go of what you have
Afraid of being wrong again
Afraid of being right
All alone at night
Feeling so cold
Wanting to lose yourself
In whatever you can
Closing yourself
To avoid yourself
Waiting for the day the light comes
And burns it all away
Will you open yourself
Will you unguard yourself
Cast away the blame
Which holds you down
Uncover your eyes
So you can see
And no longer yourself forsake

FOUR HUNDRED TWENTY

Unable to let go
Let go of this fear
For fear of falling
This doubt weighs heavy
But I am unable to cast it away
My life has brought me here
Brought me here to this place
All the grief and joy
And I am not sorry
And I hold no regrets
I am thankful
Yet I am sill unable
Unable to let go of this fear
I want to believe
I want to trust
But it is hard to forget
The truths that I have learned
And the beliefs I have seen crushed
The trials we go through
Each leaving their own scars
Memories made
Choices decided
Is it only circumstance that divides me
Each moment that passes here
Is a moment wasted here
Yet I am still unable
Unable to let go
Let go of this fear

FOUR HUNDRED TWENTY ONE

We wait until it passes
Then justify the actions
A chance
In time now past
How many are we given
To throw away
And blame our fortune
When only a finger lifted
On the road we have chosen
Comes to an end
Stuck in ourselves
We continue onward
For from ourselves we cannot bend
Then justify the actions
On presumptions made
Circumstances we cannot control
Circumstances we have let control
Our responsibilities to ourselves we let slip
With no thought beyond the present
Unexamined
Letting guilt be our guide
Blaming chance
For our choices chosen
Falling prey
To our arrogance
Taking for granted the chances
In time
Past
Mourning ourselves
In the place we hold ourselves

Resigning ourselves
Before we have even begun
Then justify our actions
In the fires of our pain
If only we can acknowledge ourselves
So we can set ourselves free
Reach out for ourselves
Reaching higher then ourselves
Believing in ourselves
Setting ourselves free

FOUR HUNDRED TWENTY TWO

When the skies darken
And the fog surrounds me
And the air is heavy
And hard to breath
Will you remind me of who I am
Will you wait for me
Until this lifts from me
Will you believe in me
When my belief falters
Will you forgive me
Until I forgive myself
I know not why I came here
And I cannot say when I will leave here
Even though I am alone here
I am not lonely here
Believing I have something to gain
Something deeper calls me here
I cannot explain this
No words can convey
I hope you can understand
But I cannot turn back now
You fear that you are losing me
All I can say is trust in me
As these insecurities and doubt
This pain and questioning are my own
I wish I could turn back
If only it were that easy
If only I could just let it go
But a purpose calls me
Far deeper than me

When the skies darken
And the fog surrounds me
And the air is heavy
And hard to breath
Will you hold the light for me
Will you wait for me

CHASING SHADOWS
(FOUR HUNDRED TWENTY FOUR)

Lend me your strength
And support me
Until I find the strength
Within myself
Finding the truth in myself
Breaking the shackles
Setting myself free
May your light fall on me
And chase the shadows from me
So I can see the fear and the doubt
So I can acknowledge them
But not become them
Will you watch over me
Until this fades from me
Like the setting of the sun
Before the dawning of a new day
I must pass through this
To awaken to a brighter day
From within
Lend me your strength
And support me
Until I find the strength
Within myself
Finding the truth in myself
Breaking the shackles
Setting myself free
May your light fall on me
And chase the shadows from me

So I can see the fear and the doubt
And not submit to them
Yet accept them
As a chance to learn from them
So I can find my way
Find my way to a brighter day
Chasing the shadows away

FOUR HUNDRED TWENTY FIVE

We chip away at ourselves
Until we accept it
Until we believe this is what we want
What we deserve
Forgetting we chipped ourselves away
Cheating ourselves
Explaining it away
Cheating each other
Justifying it away
The person we have become
We deny
Wrapping ourselves ever deeper
Ever deeper within the lie
Holding onto the promise of tomorrow
Overlooking today
And burying yesterday
To avoid the pain
Making it ever-last
Cheating ourselves
Explaining it away
Cheating each other
Justifying it away
So wrapped we become
We cannot live without
We cannot see without
Continuing the pattern
For fear we will lose ourselves
Losing our belief in ourselves
From the guilt played
Hoping for one day
Ignoring today

FOUR HUNDRED TWENTY SEVEN

When the sun recedes
And night falls
My thoughts to you I soon concede
Dreaming of you is when I feel your call
So long now has it been
Since I have felt you near
Felt your warmth
It does not feel the same
Without you here
The brightness is gone
The lightness is gone
Every second passes like an eternity
As I wait for you
And I wait for you
Without you I do not feel complete
Lost within myself
Unable to find my way home
I can almost feel you here
When the sun recedes
And night falls
My thoughts of you I soon concede
Within my thoughts of you I soon fall
As I wait for you
And I wait for you
Until we find our way home
Until we find our way
Find our way together again

FOUR HUNDRED FORTY

You did it again
It ended the same
A crying shame
Nothing left to do
But wait for the landing
This time was supposed to be different
It wasn't supposed to end the same
Shattered and broken
Dragging yourself through the shards of your heart
Again
How many second chances are you going to give
What did you think had changed
This time
Hoping in your love
This time they would be bound
Hoping in your love
This time they would be found
You did it again
It ended the same
A crying shame
Nothing left to do
But wait for the landing
Stepping forward
But going backward
Your all turned around and upside down
You did it again
It ended the same
A crying shame
Nothing left to do
But wait for the landing

They have you right where they want you
They have you right where they need you
Can you feel your heart bleeding
Again
Feeding the fear what it is needing
You did it again
It ended the same
A crying shame
Nothing left to do
But wait for the landing

FOUR HUNDRED FORTY SEVEN

When you look at me
What is it that you see
Do you want to see
Want to know what made me
What shaped me
Why it is that I flee
What it is I'm afraid of catching me
Why it's so hard for me to free
Free myself from me
Do you want to unlock the mystery
Will you chance the key
Washing away the history
White washing the memories
The memories of what made me
What shaped me
Eclipsing the negativity
Unlocking me

FOUR HUNDRED FORTY EIGHT

Before you I had nothing
And I never knew
And now your gone
And I have nothing
Oh what our hearts have been put through
But I'm not going to let you
Let you take the piece of me that inside me grew
I'm going to fight
Fight through the clouds to find the light of day
I'm not going to let you block anymore of the sun's rays
No more games to play
I'm going to find the one who cares
The one for me
The one who's love has no fee
The one who's love is free

The End